# BUILD YOUR CHARACTER ON A SOLID FOUNDATION

BY BOOKER T. MCKINSTRY'S © COPYRIGHT BY BTMS PUBLISHINGS

"Build you character on a solid foundation"

# TABLE OF CONTENTS

## FOUNDATION

Part 1. Create a roadmap (Intro) pgs. 5-7

Part 2. Set goals             pgs. 8-12

Part 3. Find balance           pg. 13

Part 4. Take action            pgs. 14-16

## HOW TO COMMUNICATE SUCCESSFULY

Part 1. What is communication? (Intro) pgs. 17-18

Part 2. What is it to communicate?     pgs. 19-20

Part 3. Word-less communication      pgs. 21-22

Part 4. Communication roadblocks     pgs. 23-24

Part 5. Communication preference?     pgs. 25-27

Part 6. How to improve harmony       pgs. 28-29

"Build you character on a solid foundation"

# CHANGE AND STRESS

Part 1. Change and stress (Intro) pg. 30
Part 2. Stress triggers          pg. 31

Part 3. Relations to stress      pgs. 32-33

Part 4. Red flags of stress      pg. 34

Part 5. Personality, stress & environment pg. 35

Part 6. How to deal             pg. 36-37

Part 7. It starts with you.      pgs. 38-42

# MONEY MANAGEMENT

Part 1. Money management (Intro)   pg. 43

Part 2. What's your view about money?  pg. 44

Part 3. Budgeting for the basics.   pgs. 45-46
Part 4. The long haul           pgs. 47-48

Part 5. Banks and debit cards    pgs. 49-50

Part 6. Loans and credit         pgs. 51-53

Part 8. Insurance               pgs. 54-56

Part 9. Home ownership          pg. 57- 59

"Build you character on a solid foundation"

# FOREWORD

This book is designed to provide practical life skills that can be used in everyday life. The authors purpose of writing this book is to consolidate much needed subjects into one compilation. These subjects are correlated towards personal development and finance. This material is only a basic knowledge of these subjects.

I believe the only thing we need in life to reach our full potential is a point in the right direction, encouragement, motivation, and the will to keep going.

Once you build you character on a solid foundation be someone's else's encouragement and motivation. A well-rounded character is something money cannot buy. Stay firm, stay solid, and live the best reality you can imagine using solid plans, skills, and the will to do.

Avoid spoiling your God given talents and abilities. Push yourself harder than ever before. Keep what you need, develop what you have, and give what you can. - BTM3

"Build you character on a solid foundation"

# SECTION 1

# FOUNDATION

"Build you character on a solid foundation"

# CREATE A ROADMAP

Nothing of important significance happens by chance. It's our ideals self-beliefs and action that get us there. If you wish to accomplish your dreams and goals it's essential to create a bright and vivid picture of what you want to attract into your life. This is one aspect of having a metaphysical experience, which is the vision of your imagination, or mind's eye.

Once the vision is set in place meditate on it. Contemplate on every detail you can imagine. involve your senses. Think of how good it feels to have what you desire. Think of how these accomplishments will bring positive changes into your life and others.

There can never be too many good reasons of why you want the things you want. Use imagination as a driving force towards your attainment. These visions are the keys to unlocking your motivation, and motivation will activate your will to manifest your visions and intentions.

Discover the powerful benefits of having a supreme imagination. Keep in mind, thoughts always come before action. Think about this question. How can you travel from one place to another without thinking

"Build you character on a solid foundation"

of that place? And how can you reach this destination without proceeding down a certain path?

If my desired destination is Florida, I cannot use California's roadmap to get there. Now, imagine driving a car that never runs out of gas, and you have no specific destination in mind. Where will you arrive? Bingo! Destination nowhere is correct.

Do not let no place be your destination. Arrive at your envisioned destiny. Clearly know what you want out of life. Envision what it looks like, how it feels, smell, or taste, metaphorically. Really put yourself there.

If your goal is to vacation in Florida. Imagine yourself laying on a beach chair relaxing, taking in the bright sun, enjoying the oceans breeze, over a tropical martini, while watching beautiful white seagulls fly overhead.

Ask yourself, why do I desire this so badly, and how will this give me great fulfilment? Once the mental aspect is covered it's time to exercise action. Put your vision in writing, plan, and work your way to achievement. Nothings comes to a dreamer but a dream. Put in the work and get the results.

"Build you character on a solid foundation"

## SET GOALS

Setting goals are creating plans perfectly aligned with your vision. Basic goal setting can be characterized under these four common categories: personal goals, advancement goals, career goals, and charitable goals.

Personal goals concerns family, friends, or anything involving your personal life. Being a better parent, spending more time with your spouse, reaching out to friends, or even, taking a trip to Vegas or the Caribbean's are examples.

Always strive and be the best you possible. Live according to your true potential and remember quality always earn more and achieve more. Cheap things break easily. Be sure of making it your business to nurture your strongest qualities, and use strength to overcome your most detrimental weaknesses. All weakness must go, especially those weaknesses blocking the gateway of your destiny.

Advancement goals. These goals are geared towards new skill training, or enhancing the skills and ability you currently possess. Maintaining and further developing your skill set marks the difference of amateurs and professionals.

"Build you character on a solid foundation"

Entry level pay in comparison to branch management pay; regional managers salary in comparison to national mangers salary. The point is this. Each level of promotion involves different elements of knowledge or expertise. If you build your skills, more people will seek your service over your competitors and many major corporations pay top dollar for specialized knowledge and skills. Your expertise makes you valuable. This is your bargaining leverage. Therefore, never sell yourself short.

Career goals. Career goals can be dreams of being a nurse, or a businessman with the intention of earning more money for your family. You may set a goal to increase your yearly salary from $30,000 annually to $30,000 monthly. Whatever your career goals are, achieve them by staying focused and passionate.

Charitable goals are what you plan to do around your community. This can be giving a donation, or volunteering your time to your favorite charity. If you recognize a void in your community that you can fill, fill it! Or even, create a foundation of your own if you have a good idea.

Being active in the community helps you stay grounded, and it is counted respectable or noble of the person willing to reach down and pull others up. To whom much is given much is required of him/her. It is better to give than to receive because the giver produces, and the receiver consumes. And I will say, it is better to have something to give than it is to have nothing to live.

"Build you character on a solid foundation"

In addition to goal categories there are timeframes. and these timeframes are: long-term, mid-term, and short-term.

Long-term goals can take up to 5yrs. or longer to accomplish. For instance, maybe your aiming to be a doctor, or maybe you're working on a master's degree.

Mid-term goals are more than 1yr; but less than 5yrs. Maybe you're working towards a bachelor's degree.

Short-term goals are less than 1yr., like a plumbing certificate, or even an air-conditioning and heating certificate.

Listen. please understand everyone has aspired wishes and dreams to make something of themselves, but so few are willing to move pass the state of inspiration. Having a clear vision is well and dandy, but solely thinking will not bring forth its manifestation. The only way to manifest your ideals quickly is through consistent action. Inconsistent action is delay, and delay is decay. Opportunities do not last a lifetime, they speedily come and quickly vanish.

Make the first move, write a plan. Many may say, "I don't need a plan," or "I have the plan in my mind." I thought the same way at one point in my life. Even though, written plans are not mandatory to achieve your objectives, however somethings absolutely need planning in order to accomplish

"Build you character on a solid foundation"

effectively. In these examples, I will further explicate.

I could not help but analyze the fact that, a building contractor needs a blueprint from the architect and the laborers need these measurements of the blueprint from the contractor. The teacher needs a curriculum, and the pastor needs a sermon. Now, picture writing your name without ever seeing its description. Ah hah! In essence, this is exactly what we ask our sub-conscious mind to do for our conscience mind, which is to act with no instruction manual.

I cannot over emphasize the importance of writing your steps of projected achievement down on paper, constantly revising them along the way, if necessary. Your plans are your lamp post. Make your plans bright and vivid, let them become a part of your being. Planning will help you keep a razor-sharp focus. Overlook your goals daily. State your goals to yourself and your supporters with excitement. Use strong phrases of faith and belief, with no wavering thoughts of doubt. "I will have the best", "I will not be denied", "I was born for this day". Claim it with the power of confirmation. Articulate phrases like, "I will be very wealthy" rather than" I will not be poor".

These affirmations will ignite or strengthen electrical charges in your body and your mind that is needed to believe and act upon that belief. You can't fake belief or faith. Our actions generally reflect our

"Build you character on a solid foundation"

most dominate thoughts and beliefs. Imagination is our virtual reality. Working and achieving the results of our imagination, or mind's eye are the physical manifestation of our thoughts.

Track your progress. Project the exact time, in which you wish to reach your achievements. Will it be in 5years, 3 years, 6 months, 1 week you decide? Remember, setting deadlines puts the game in motion.

Nurture your dreams, don't be discouraged, and adjust your plans when necessary. Work on each type of goal daily to avoid neglecting one over another. Keep in mind, enhancing your abilities helps you earn more, and earning more helps you do more; for yourself, family, friends, and community. Writing your plan on paper will give you a detailed strategy of how to help yourself.

"Build you character on a solid foundation"

# FIND BALANCE

Be sure all your aims in life are driven from within. Your dreams do not belong to your parents, significant other, best friend, or grandmother. What someone else says, matters not concerning your life.

You and only you must own your ambitions. If your dreams are not truly yours, lack of motivation will arise, and you will have trouble coercing your body to obey your mind. If it's something you truly desire to have you will certainly find the drive, passion, and determination to press forward.

Make your goals manageable. Divide long-term goals into mid-term increments, break mid-term goals down into short-term parts, and reduce short-term goals into increments of months, weeks, days, hours, minutes, and seconds, if needed

. There is no such thing as extra time. Make your existence count.

"Build you character on a solid foundation"

## TAKE ACTION

Avoid procrastination, excuses, and fear. These three elements are enemies of action. They are your most pivotal opposition that must be subdued and conquered.

Generally, peoples' main excuses for not acting is the lack of time or fear. But let's face it we spend a lot time following people on the internet and television follow their dreams, rather than utilizing this time working on important task of our own.

Observe yourself, notice where your overspending fruitful time on matters of unimportance. Wasted time is the withering of life. Do not live the unfulfilling life, the life of regret. The life of not reaching your fullest potential. Time is limited, so determine a start line and finish line. Begin your game.

If you need help getting started, list and tackle the small task first, or simply do anything in connection to your objective.

Set aside a portion of each day to attack your goals. Most of us have high energy portions of our day. Utilize this part of day for your most important difficult task. You may have to give up or cut down on things you really like, or cherish doing for the sake of making time for the purpose of receiving the

"Build you character on a solid foundation"

things you truly want out of life. Less television, social media, or beauty sleep maybe all the extra time you need without sacrificing your entire life. But, be willing to do whatever it takes under reasonable ground to get the job done.

Keep the end results in mind, stay encouraged. Let acting towards your goals be your most dominating thoughts. Prioritize your steps and be accurate about how long each goal will take. Reward yourself when you cross a milestone. Share your progress with your support system, make them feel a part of the process. If they truly wish you well, then receive their well wishes graciously. This will help you maintain high enthusiasm. Support systems are great to have, but the lack thereof, should not make or break you. Ultimately, you are your support.

Prioritize. In some cases, one task can't be started until first completing another. For example, before operating an 18-wheeler you must first obtain your CDL permit.

Do not let fear stop you. Some of the most successful people have failed multiple times over. But eventually they prevailed. And you likewise can and will prevail if you don't faint. Keep going and finish. Nobody wants to lose, but you can't win if you don't play.

Again, writing, detailing, and, acting on your vision is the sure way to achieving. Stay excited about your vision and don't be too hard on yourself. If you fall

"Build you character on a solid foundation"

off track, hop back on preferably quickly, but never the less, get back on and keep riding.

Motivation. There are two basic types of motivation. "I want" and "I don't want". When you like doing something, like a hobby, playing sports video games, hanging out with the guys, or family you don't need persuasion. It is not necessary to twist your arm for you to eat your favorite ice cream.

Doing things, you'd rather not takes more effort or persuasion. For example, most kids do not like eating vegetables, so for persuasion, the kids parent may threaten to withhold dessert or other privileges if the child refuses to comply. Tomorrow you may need a different dessert.

Often you will encounter difficult challenges in life, so stay aware and minimize these setbacks. Before dedicating time and resources for the attainment of a goal, ask yourself "Am I willing to endure all the work required to receive my reward? Am I willing to exhaust my resources to reach my destiny.

Hard work pays off, so get busy.

"Build you character on a solid foundation"

# SECTION 2

# HOW TO COMMUNICATE SUCCESSFULLY

"Build you character on a solid foundation"

## COMMUNICATION

Communication is a learned skill that starts from birth, or even before birth as an embryo. This skill is further developed throughout our lifelong span of interactions with other people. As we grow and become better communicators, we gain more social awareness. Meaning, we learn to confer and hear the message intended to be given or received.

Most us take verbal communication for granted. But, as we began to make friends, or converse with family and friends we began to understand the importance of the spoken word, and begin to speak with intention and hear for understanding. Perfecting this skill gives us the ability to develop required communication skills to form good relationships in our social, personal, and professional life.

Failing to develop a healthy social life can lead to self-isolation, which can also cause serious health issues mental and physical. The fact of the matter is, we all need other people because we all are social beings. To understand and be understood we must learn to effectively communicate with all ethnic groups and cultures. In all thy getting get

"Build you character on a solid foundation"

understanding. Understanding is everything. Be slow to speak, swift to hear, and slow to anger.

## WHAT IS IT TO COMMUNICATE?

Knowing the science of communication is the first step to becoming a great communicator.

Communication is the transfer of messages. These messages can be written words, facial expressions or body language. The components of communication consist of a sender, receiver, and the message. The sender sends the message and the receiver interprets the message. If the sender and receiver understands the same message effective communication has occurred.

The two main patterns of communication are one-way communication and two-way communication. One -way communication is when the sender sends the message and the receiver receives the message with no reply.

Two-way communication is when the receiver understands the message and responds with another message. One-way communication is fast and straight to the point, no curves, and no turns. This method of communing is normally used by leaders. Typically, when your boss gives you an order, the

"Build you character on a solid foundation"

expectation is that you follow the command with no response, whether it be negative or positive. This form of communication gives lead way for many misinterpretations.

On the other hand, two-way communication gives the opportunity of clarifying the message assumed to be understood.

Clarification eradicates or limits misunderstandings, so if you don't fully understand the message being delivered don't pretend to comprehend, ask for clarity. "Never travel the path of no direction."

"Build you character on a solid foundation"

# WORDLESS COMMUNICATION

Most people think the main method of communication are with words, even though what we say and how we say it is very important, research has proven that 85% of communication is non-verbal. It is easier to disguise the way you feel with your words, but body language and facial expressions are much harder to control.

Be aware of your facial expressions. Most facial expressions are universal, cultural background does not matter. Gestures of frowning, smiling, and raising your eyebrows are just a few. Facial expressions are the major indicator of feelings, so be careful not to deliver the wrong message. Deliver your messages in the way you want them perceived. Remember nobody truly knows how you feel on the inside.

People can only assess your words, body language, and actions. Be sure to deliver the correct facial message, even though it can be difficult.

I must point to the fact that; all smiling faces are not equivalent to being nice or happy. And likewise, all frowns doesn't indicate mean or angry. And moreover, smiles and nods doesn't always mean the listener agrees with you.

If people only hear 10% of what you say, then the other 90% is used thinking of a reply. But how can

"Build you character on a solid foundation"

you make an accurate response if the message was not fully heard? Right there, is the breakdown in communication. Pay attention. These people do not listen to understand, they hear to oppose. Therefore, we cannot always dictate a person's true feelings or intentions through body language or facial expressions. People express themselves in various ways, so get to know the person before assuming. Let's get more in depth on this subject of discussion.

## COMMUNICATION ROADBLOCKS

Remember successful communication means that both the receiver and the sender understands the message. The message and its delivery must be clear and concise. Say what you mean and hear what's being said. Miscommunication derives from physical, mental, or emotional roadblocks. If miscommunication occurs, be sure to examine yourself to ensure you're not blocking the message.

Physical roadblocks are environmental distractions that alters successful communication. Noisy places, and many other background distractions can cause ineffective communication. Even discomfort in your posture of standing or sitting can cause you to

"Build you character on a solid foundation"

misinterpret the message being delivered at that point of the interference.

Mental roadblocks are when the receiver hears the message and automatically relate comparisons in their mind of something they know to make since of the message.

For example, a doctor explaining open heart surgery to a person that has no medical background, or someone that has no general understanding of medical terminology. Under this circumstance the sender must be able to deliver the message in a way it can be understandable.

Emotional roadblocks can prevent communication if a person is in opposition with the message based on their values and self-belief system. In this circumstance they will automatically reject the message, so it will be better to agree to disagree. It's not worth the battle because most people are slow to let go of their well-defined personal belief systems, even if their beliefs are inaccurate.

Other mental roadblocks can derive from worries and fears. The receiver may be dealing with tough situations in his\her own personal lives and can in consequence tremendously take a negative effect on one's ability to focus, understand, and interpret the message being delivered. It is important to have a clear and unbiased opinion to thoroughly receive and understand a message, because your message will not penetrate or enter a distracted, or closed mind.

"Build you character on a solid foundation"

Communication roadblocks drives wedges between all parties involved, causing a lack of rapport or harmony between the receiver and the sender. This resorts into ineffective communication.

## WHATS YOUR COMMUNICATION PREFERENCE?

The main staple in communicating effectively is knowing who you are, and it is also especially important to be aware of the people or person you converse with. Pay attention to their feelings, needs, and personality. Deal with people in alignment to their personalities. This will dramatically increase your chances of receiving a positive response from them. Your understanding of them will cause them to understand you in return. This creates harmony amongst you both and with harmony understanding is achieved.

There are many basic communication styles, but I will discuss the four common ones. The seller, relator, achiever, and thinker.

Thinking people have great self-control and they generally, guard themselves from others doing interactions. They tend not to tell very much about

"Build you character on a solid foundation"

themselves and would rather ask questions about your concerns and interest.

Achievers are like thinkers they both have great self-control and are as well, very guarded. The contrast is that achievers are far more expressive about what they want or expect and are sure to be understood.

The sellers style of communication demonstrates charisma, which displays an outgoing spirit. These people get along with everyone. They are very friendly in nature, they express themselves forcefully and assertively.

The relaters style. The relaters style expresses warmth and friendliness. Their main concern are other people. We normally consider these people as nosey because they absolutely must know every tedious detail about any situation. They will even ask personal questions expecting answers and will become upset if you wish to be conservative.

Everyone has a preferred style of communicating. Depending on the person, it may be necessary to adjust your style of communicating. No conversation is the same, similar maybe, but not the same. This is one major reason of why it's wise to be aware of people's emotions and communication styles.

Timing is everything. If you catch someone at a bad time, you will likely not have a pleasant discussion, so," back off!" As an upset person, would say.

"Build you character on a solid foundation"

If you intercede with your supervisor it may be more appropriate to be a thinker, being careful not to put a foot in your mouth.

If it's an idea you wish to complete you will operate as an achiever.

Maybe your marketing a new product to a potential client, then you will use the sellers style.

If your interacting with a close friend or family member, then in this case, you are relating.

Successful communication is essential to creating positive relationships and favorable circumstances in your life. Misinterpretations of messages results into misunderstandings and disharmony.

"Build you character on a solid foundation"

## HOW TO IMPROVE HARMONY?

Understand. If communication styles were automatically harmonious people would not have misunderstandings, which in some cases leads to death. So here are a few basic ways to create harmonious relationships and improve disharmonious communications. Slightly adjusting to the other person's communication style can greatly improve the nature of communication because most people relate to others whom share the same personality.

For example, if someone is speaking to you in a low soft tone, maybe you should respond in that same low soft tone. If the sender constantly maintains eye contact do the same, maintain eye contact. The majority perceive lack of eye contact as lack of concern. Using the same hand gestures and facial expressions are other examples.

For respect sake, do not imitate or mimic a person every move this could be obvious and annoying and therefore, will not create harmony.

If you're a little shy and have a problem with breaking the ice a little small talk one 101 will take you along way.

"Build you character on a solid foundation"

The simplest way to engage with people is to create small talk. Small talk is more effective if the topic is based on an interest you both have knowledge about.

This can also be a time of learning. Per say, you have an interest in becoming a businessman and you have an opportunity to engage with a successful business person. The wisest thing to do is listen, and speak sparingly. If the appropriate time presents itself speak but be sure your statements are short, brief, appropriate, and sensible. If you are a master student seeking knowledge, ask questions.

"Build you character on a solid foundation"

# SECTION 3

# CHANGE
# AND
# STRESS

"Build you character on a solid foundation"

## CHANGE AND STRESS

Change is necessary for growth, and it's nearly impossible to reach your full potential without realizing this fact.

Can you imagine an adult crawling upon the floor like an infant asking you to play with him or her? Being unable to handle change causes stress, which is the psychological or physical response. This is when a person has difficulty managing stressful events, situations, or change in their life.

Understand stressful situations are not all equivalent, problems do vary in degree. One person's tremendous stress could be another person's happy challenge. For example, some people fear snakes, but other people adore them. They even let them slither around their neck and arms giggling and smiling.

Although, long-term stress can cause serious health issues, stress can also have its good side, if you learn to channel this resource into power instead of destroying yourself. Use this power to propel you towards your destiny, when tough challenges arrive take a moment to recollect your thoughts before

"Build you character on a solid foundation"

responding. Dealing with stress in a sensible way will save you a lot of heartache.

## STRESS TRIGGERS

Major, minor, daily, and catastrophic situations are stress triggers. Major situations are like, a loved one passing away, or your home going into foreclosure, or a person losing their high-paying job, or even having a life-threatening disease.

Minor situations are like being late for a meeting or not paying a late parking ticket.

Catastrophic situations are terrorist attacks, major earthquakes, or even category 5 hurricanes.

Unpredictable situations are more stressful than predictable situations. Every stress trigger falls under one of these core categories and each category has a different level of intensity. An unpredictable situation causes more stress than a predictable situation, like being fired from your employment, rather than quitting.

Indefinite thoughts are more stressful than definite thoughts, like not knowing if you have the winning lottery ticket for $300 million dollars.

Some long-term problems can cause more stress than short-term problems. Having a terminal disease is more stressful than a broken arm.

"Build you character on a solid foundation"

Stress can make you feel helpless, and if not handled properly, stress can make you lose control of your ability to think and act sensibly possibly provoking loss of temperament, so recognize the signs and do what it takes to keep your composure. This feeling of helplessness can lead to suicide, so if your struggles feel overwhelming to the point you wish to cause bodily harm to yourself or someone else seek help. Reach out to people that really cares about your well-being. And if no one is available just think about all the positive people in your life and how they will be negatively affected for life. You are somebody, and only you can be that somebody for them.

"Build you character on a solid foundation"

## REACTIONS TO STRESS

Everyone reacts to stress differently, but it will be psychological or physical. In my opinion, it's a combination of both.

Psychological reactions promote these following physical reactions. We ask ourselves is this good or bad? Can I handle this situation? Or, what will happen if I can't provide a sufficient solution, or how will this affect my self-belief system?

Automatic physical responses require high hormone levels, which produces high-blood pressure, faster heart rate, and more energy. These reactions give you the ability to combat the problem or surrender. We use all our abilities to manage difficulties for some while, but if the problem persists we usually give in.

Exposure to long-term stress can break down your mental and physical health. Physically this includes the weakening of your body's ability to fight against sickness or infections.

Psychologically you can have trouble performing daily task like war veterans, or victims of a traumatic crime. When stress is around, anxiety is sure to be somewhere nearby.

"Build you character on a solid foundation"

# RED FLAGS OF STRESS

Physical signs of stress are non-exercise related muscle tensions in your neck or shoulders. Stress can also cause chest pains, sleepiness, headaches, high blood pressure, and a wide range of other physical break downs in your body.

Stress will also change the way you see and think about things in your life. Lack of focus, confusion, constant negative thoughts, non-stop thinking, and indecision are mental signs of stress.

The emotional side of stress can be depression, fear, frustration, nervousness, anxiety, and anger. These feelings create short-tempers and high irritability. This generally festers into behavioral issues such as, cursing, blaming others, smoking, drinking, crying uncontrollably, pacing, nail-biting, hitting, throwing things, and yelling. If you conduct yourself in this manner, consider the way these negative actions will impact your life.

"Build you character on a solid foundation"

# PERSONALITY, STRESS, & ENVIROMENT

What's your attitude towards change? Some people welcome change, whereas others may despise or resist this nudging energy. Beware, some people may become overwhelmed and fall by the wayside.

Here are some key factors that increases stress levels. Not desiring to change or take calculated risk; low self-esteem, weak coping, weak money management skills, or lack of social support.

On the other hand, self-belief, change, risk, courage, coping, good money management skills, and a supportive social network can protect us from stress.

Many people are afraid of change because of the unknown, so they would rather do what they've always done to have what they've always had. For these people doing something new, different, and out of routine makes them very nervous and uncomfortable.

Overly cautious people have a hard time altering their self-belief. They will go to the extreme to resist making change, or taking risk. This does them more harm than good because their stress level increases.

"Build you character on a solid foundation"

This is the thing, we all must understand that change is inevitable, it's a part of our continuous life cycle. Do your best to encourage positive thoughts. Positive thoughts encourage change, so embrace change as a challenge not an opposition.

"Build you character on a solid foundation"

# HOW TO DEAL

Strong people believe in their ability to control and manage their lives. They also feel strongly about their ability to influence their environment and not be influenced by it. Consequently, over confident people feel the need to control everything, and if something isn't going according to their plan they become very stressed.

Having balance and good temperament is important. No person wants to feel helpless and no human being is all-powerful. Study and learn yourself, be aware of your triggers and potential reactions. The knowing and control of self is the best and most rewarding riches or wisdom you can ever receive.

# IT STARTS WITH YOU

The first thing you must thoroughly understand is yourself. To get along with other people you must know yourself. Whether you agree or not how other people see you is a major component to be considered. Your values, beliefs, attitudes, and emotions are the cornerstones of who you are.

How you operate in each of these different states of mind will determine how others relate to you.

"Build you character on a solid foundation"

Remember people with high self-esteem believe they can create their own destiny, so they truly believe that they can influence circumstances to bring any objective into its full conception.

Once you began to believe in yourself it becomes easier to believe in others. When you arrive to the realization of who you are, you will understand that you are not better than anyone else, and that everyone is unique in their own way. So therefore, there is no need to be in competition with fellow human beings.

The key to good relationships are respect, trust, and understanding. These qualities promote pleasant relations. Good relationships equal good communication and a healthy social life.

Being someone's friend does not give you a pass to accuse, demean, or be sarcastic towards them. These types of situations can create friction, and over a long period of time will develop into resentment, and resentment will manifest into bad relations.

However, most relationships have disagreements from time to time. But how you handle these disagreements is what dictates the outcome of the relationships of friends, spouses, strangers, coworkers and so on.

Assertiveness. Its ok and necessary to express your honest opinion to others. But you must use discretion, especially if your statement is not considered positive. Consider how you would feel if you were in

"Build you character on a solid foundation"

that person's shoes. No matter how uncompassionate someone may pretend to be, at the end of day, everyone has feelings and emotions. Your emotions may be suppressed, but they are there. So be sure to treat people with dignity and respect. Never forget, people always remember the way you made them feel, status does not matter. Let's face it most people like people that like them. Remember when giving feedback to others, take account of your own feelings. To help with this, consider what motivates you. Do not judge or pressure the other person to reveal information about themselves. Do not harshly criticize their decisions or their way of doing things. Only give feedback if you can help solve the problem, but don't tell them what to do. Be articulate with your choice of words because some people put up self- defense mechanisms before the first word is spoken.

Here's a description of a few defense mechanisms, starting with withdrawal. This mechanism avoids the situation altogether. These people prefer not to talk about stressful things.

Another defense mechanism is rationalization. This mechanism is used when people use excuses, in attempt to explain their way out of a situation.

Then we have displacement. This reaction is expressed angrily, or expressed through anxiety.

"Build you character on a solid foundation"

These are typically, the in your face, with arms flinging type of people, which is considered the lowest level of self-control. This mechanism is usually attached to people with low income and low self-esteem. Fantasy or daydreams provide self-confidence if you're not confident in real life.

Lastly, is projection. The person using this mechanism will go tick for tack with no intention of resolution in mind. Constantly being on defense makes it difficult, if not impossible to change and grow. Defensive people have trust issues and are afraid to let others into their personal lives because they fear criticism. On the other hand, open minded people can accept constructive criticism and in return they receive growth in progression and develop more meaningful relationships. To further help you avoid emotional defensiveness, examine the examiner, and if this person is truly certified about what's being spoken, it may be worth giving a hearing ear.

Another strategy is to listen to the words verses the tone of voice. I know some people can get under your skin with their sharp criticisms, these criticisms can literally pierce a person's soul, but as the old saying goes" The truth hurts", so take the positive words and leave the negative tone out. If none of it is true don't fight or argue, just simply remove yourself from your accuser, or just simply ignore them all together.

Another way is to take your time before responding. Take a deep breath. Give that initial rush of uneasiness time to pass over. The more skilled you

"Build you character on a solid foundation"

are at not becoming entangled with negative feelings and emotions, the higher possibility you have at creating a tremendously healthy social life.

"Build you character on a solid foundation"

Stay Solid

# SECTION 4

# MONEY MANAGEMENT

"Build you character on a solid foundation"

## MONEY MANAGEMENT

I must emphasize it takes money to survive and reach our hopes and dreams. The lack of money is the number one factor blocking most our ability to enjoy ourselves and the people around us.

Surviving is having your basic needs, like a place to rest your head, food to eat, and clothing to put on your back. Money and time is a limited resource, so it's always to our best interest to manage them both with precise accuracy, quickly propelling you to reach your destiny. The secret to building wealth is simple. Spend less than you have and multiply what you don't spend. Believe in your power to do, and it will be given to you.

"Build you character on a solid foundation"

# WHATS YOUR VIEW ABOUT MONEY

Money creates positive, or negative emotions for many adults. If we have the things we need and desire, we feel a sense of security and self-empowerment. In contrast, the lack of money causes us to feel angry and upset. Our self-belief determines the way we feel about money.

In many cultures success is greatly based upon material possessions. Many people let money determine their inner worth. But I must say to be clearly understood, having money and nice things are great, but it will never be a solid positive foundation for a positive self-belief. Like the time worn cliché proceeds, "money cannot buy happiness". Remember money is obtained on the outside and happiness always comes from within.

"Build you character on a solid foundation"

## BUDGETING FOR THE BASICS

Strategizing or writing down a calculated plan of how you will spend your money is called budgeting. A budget is a strategy about how you spend your money towards your short-term, mid-term, or long-term financial goals. The purpose of a budget is to help prevent overspending in unwarranted areas, and if followed will guide you to use your money for the purpose of your intention.

The important benefits of strategizing are knowing exactly how much money you have or earn, and knowing exactly how you intend to distribute this precious resource. Creating a solid financial strategy forces you to focus on your priorities and goals, so stick to the plan and build wealth.

Let's talk about income and expenses. Income is the money you earn. Earning income can be achieved in numerous ways, general society typically earn their income through employment, running their business, or hobbies of some sort. Some people work for a company and themselves. If you are like most people you know where your money comes from.

Every cent of income received before deductions is called gross income. If you work for a company federal taxes are normally deducted automatically

"Build you character on a solid foundation"

from your earnings, along with any other voluntary deductions, such as 401k plans, insurance and so forth. After these deductions, your left with your take home pay or remaining income which is called your net income. For some people making money is not a problem, keeping track of where it disappears is their million-dollar question.

The last statement brings me to expenses. Any place you spend your money without receiving an equivalent or higher rate of return in exchange is called and expense. Expenses can vary. Expenses heavily depends on our personal lifestyles, and the lifestyles of the people in which we are responsible for. Some people have fixed expenses. This means their total expenses and due dates are the same year-round which is more convenient for those with fixed incomes. Fixed expenses can be car note payments, rent, cable television, mortgage, or any expense that never changes.

Expenses that varies each month, quarter, or year are called variable expenses. For example, entertainment, gas, car and home repairs, furniture, food, and clothing...

Note this one thing for certainty. If your expenses outweigh the amount of income you earn you are in big financial trouble. However, you can fix this money problem via strategized planning and swift execution. Income is earned not given.

"Build you character on a solid foundation"

# THE LONG HAUL

If you plan to start your own business, or pay for your children's college education you will need a substantial amount of money. Let's face it, it is hard to earn large sums of income in today's workplace, without having some specialized skill or bachelor's degree. I am not saying it's impossible, everything is possible, but putting money aside for the long haul is just something many are not currently able to achieve.

The last thing young people are thinking of is retirement. Struggling parents of a newborn baby may think about pampers rather than putting income away for their babies' college tuition. The truth is this, no matter what circumstances may be in your way the fact remains that the earlier you invest in your future the sooner you will reap the reward. Earn more income, spend less money, or do both, if you truly wish to get ahead financially.

Home ownership is a common way to save money for the long haul, another way is through purchasing stock. Purchasing stock allows you to become part owner of the corporation. Generally, you are paid dividends when a company does well, or you can

"Build you character on a solid foundation"

trade stocks. Keep in mind you can also lose money stock investing, especially if you buy stocks from new companies. If you are interested in learning about stock investing contact a financial advisor.

Index funding. Index funding is one of the best ways to go, because this type of stock invests in all companies. Index funds gives the best return rate over the long-term.

Bonds are less risky than stocks, which in turn generate less profits. Bonds invests your money and pay you on the maturity date with interest.

Mutual funds pool a group of people money together and make investments on their behalf. Mutual funds can be strictly stock funds, bond funds, funds, or a combination of them all.

SEPS, 401k plans, and IRA plans are generally for retirement. These plans are invested in mutual funds and banks.

Education savings accounts. These accounts are initiatives for you to continue your education and these accounts also grow tax-free when used for educational purposes.

These plans stated above are not FDIC insured, so take caution when investing your money. Build a good relationship with a banker representative, or a finance broker of an established firm. Do not put all your eggs into one basket, it is better to diversify your investments because diversifying helps you offset potential losses.

"Build you character on a solid foundation"

## BANKS AND DEBIT CARDS

Most people don't feel safe walking around with large sums of cash, so we tend to keep most of our income in a bank or credit union. When choosing a financial institution, be sure your money is FDIC insured. Compare interest rates with other banks and credit institutions before committing. Be sure to ask how your money will be accessible. And ask, if that institution offers different accounts. And if so, what are the maintenance fees?

Sometimes it's better to open more than one checking account. Most people use checking accounts for holding money and making financial transactions, like ATM withdrawals etc.

Savings accounts pay compound interest on the amounts you deposit and the rates can vary from bank to bank. To determine how long it will take to double your invested income, divide 72% by the rate of your banks interest rate. This total is the dividends your money will earn annually.

Passbook accounts requires a small deposit and pays a small interest.

Money market accounts require a minimum balance and there maybe specifications on withdrawals.

"Build you character on a solid foundation"

Certificate of deposits pay high interest rates, but you must hold the certificate for the agreed amount of time. If you choose to withdraw your money before the stated maturity date you may have to pay a stiff penalty.

IRA accounts are individual retirement accounts. Likewise, early withdrawals equal penalties.

Debit cards. Debit card purchases are automatically deducted from your checking or savings account. Most debit cards do not allow you to make purchases over the balance available in your account. However, some banks and credit unions do not provide overdraft protection. In which, the financial institution will not honor overdrafts. These transactions also carry stiff penalties.

"Build you character on a solid foundation"

# LOANS AND CREDIT

Spend now pay later. Loans are money borrowed from a lender. Lenders typically charge interest on the principal borrowed at a specific interest rate. Loans can be a lifesaver if you are sinking in debt and need a quick fix to get back on your feet, or to take care of unforeseen expenses.

Loans also allows you to buy large ticket items, like purchasing a car, house, or for starting or expanding a business. Making your payments on time is vital to receiving future loans from your current lender or other lenders. Payment history is a major factor of calculating your FICA score, and your FICA score is a major determinate traditional banks and credit unions use to determine loan qualifications. If you cannot afford it, then do not take out a loan. Lenders can repossess anything you purchase, if you do not meet the contracted payments.

Receiving loans can be easy and enticing, but the inability to pay in a timely manner will quickly have your head buried in debt. The cost of loans can be expensive in the long haul, so be smart and shop around for the lowest interest rates or APR.

"Build you character on a solid foundation"

A.P.R is the money added in addition to the original principal. Never agree to terms and conditions that you do not fully understand.

Types of loans. Let's start with personal loans. Personal loans are usually used for large purchases like starting a business, or buying a home.

Student loans. There are many student loans, but the most basic are federal student loans. These loans are subsidized, meaning you are not required to pay them back until after you graduate. Considering you will become employed in your career and pay it back. These loans are insured by the government in case of default.

Private lenders offer student loans as well, but because this money is not insured interest rates are usually much higher.

Installment loans payments are on the same day each month. Refrain from taking more than one installment loan at a time. This will help you maintain a high credit score.

Where can you get a loan? Credit unions, banks, loan companies, loan sharks, private lenders, or family members. At all cost try to never and I mean never take out a payday loan the interest rates are extremely horrendous and are almost impossible to repay. If you get in over your head, you will never see your paycheck again.

"Build you character on a solid foundation"

How to build credit? Apply for a small installment loan, if someone will co-sign for you. Another way to receive a loan for establishing credit is with collateral, this can even be cash. You can receive a secured credit card as well if you use your own cash. Your money is the security. Building excellent credit takes time so be patient. It takes from six months up to one year to build a solid credit history.

Credit and installment payments are reported to the 3 major credit bureaus, Equifax, Transunion, and Experian. The credit scale ranges from very poor to excellent. A good credit rating starts from 650 and upwards. Scores below 650 are considered a risk, which raises the cost of borrowing money.

Good to excellent credit scores has the lowest interest rates. If you fall behind on your payments reach out to the lender, create a plan of action, and fulfill your obligations.

Manage your money. Do not borrow unless it is necessary. this is the key to staying out of debt. Be sure to keep a record of how much money you spend and earn.

Credit cards. Credit cards allows you make purchases up to the limit amount. This is called a credit limit. When timely payments are made towards a credit card it goes back towards your available balance, which can be used towards future purchases.

Take note, unlike loans credit card purchases can be interest free if you have a 0-statement balance before

"Build you character on a solid foundation"

the new billing cycle begins. If you can't pay the balance in full the remaining balance will be susceptible to the APR interest. Be careful, loans and credit cards are not free money, so be sure to use it wisely.

## INSURANCE

Insurance is very useful and can be used for many different purposes. There are many types of insurances, but I will address, medical, health, auto, disability, renters, and homeowners' insurance.

Medical insurance is used when we have an accident or become sick and unable to work.

Traditional health insurance covers 80% of your medical expenses. With this type of insurance, you pay your medical expenses upfront and the insurance company reimburses you the difference. This insurance is more expensive because you can choose the hospital of your choice.

Managed care plans are like traditional health insurance. The difference is that you are restricted from your personal choice of hospitals, and you must use a doctor within the network provided under your

"Build you character on a solid foundation"

provider's plan. This coverage is more affordable then traditional health care.

Medicaid and Medicare. Medicaid is for the poor and Medicare is for the disabled or elderly. Some states provide this service for free or at very low cost for children.

Auto insurance. Most states require you have maintain liability insurance at the minimum. This type of insurance covers you if someone's property is damaged while operating a motor vehicle.

Insurance policies can be upgraded. Collision and comprehensive coverage are common upgrades. Collision coverage repairs damages to your car. Most insurance companies require you to pay $500 or an $250 deductible. Deductibles are the initial payment needed to start on repairs. Any amount for repairs above your deducted cost is covered by your insurance carrier. Keep in mind your insurance company will not pay more than your car is worth.

Comprehensive insurance protects your car, if its stolen, catches fire, becomes flooded etc. If your car is old and does not have very much value I recommend liability only. Collision and comprehensive insurance will be wasting your money.

Medical coverage is for injuries. Uninsured motorist coverage protects you if you are killed or injured, or if your car is damaged by someone without insurance.

"Build you character on a solid foundation"

Some states have no fault insurance. This insurance takes care of you and the other driver regardless of who's at fault. Insurance premiums are always higher for young urban drivers because of high risk. Be sure to shop around before making your final choice. Your policy rate will be lower if you buy a less expensive or, used car. Cars with alarm systems, anti-theft systems, air bags, and other important safety features will lower policy rates as well. Keep in mind high deductible coverage are less expensive than low deductible plans.

Insurance companies provide discounts for good students. And lower rates are available for those that completes an approved driver's education course. This is called a good drivers discount.

Renters insurance protects your property against damage or loss.

Life insurance provides financial protection in the case of death. Funeral expenses and so forth.

Disability insurance pays you a certain amount of money, if you become injured or too sick to work.

Lastly, long-term care insurance provides coverage for long nursing home stays.

"Build you character on a solid foundation"

## HOME OWNERSHIP

The benefit of home ownership. When you take out a mortgage to pay for your home, a major percentage or 100% of each mortgage payment is equity paid toward ownership of that home.

For example, if your home is valued at $200,000 and you have $25,000 in equity you own 25% of the home. Many people consider their homes equity to be a savings for retirement.

The insurance and property taxes you pay towards your home are tax-deductible. Once you own your home or have a significant amount of equity in it, you can then use this property as collateral.

Financing a home usually requires a down payment of 5% to 20% of the purchase price if you choose to finance. Be sure that you thoroughly understand the terms and condition of the mortgage contract before signing.

Be sure not to accept balloon mortgages or teaser rates. These mortgage payments can skyrocket during the life-time of the mortgage, so be sure if possible to buy your property when the market value is low. Before buying a home consider all the

"Build you character on a solid foundation"

additional cost; maintenance, property taxes, insurance, repairs any many unforeseeable expenses.

Establish your credit. Earn a substantial income, and build your dream home!

"Build you character on a solid foundation"

# BUILD YOUR CHARACTER ON A SOLID FOUNDATION

BY BOOKER T. MCKINSTRY'S © COPYRIGHT BY BTMS PUBLISHINGS

"Build you character on a solid foundation"

Made in the
USA
Lexington, KY